Lean Marketing Approach

**More leads Increased revenue
Reduced advertising.**

Koso Brown

Copyright 2024© Koso Brown

All rights reserved. This book is copyrighted and no part of it may be reproduced, distributed, or transmitted in any form or by any means, including photocopying, recording, or other electronic or mechanical methods, without the prior written permission of the publisher, except in the case of brief quotations embodied in critical reviews and certain other non-commercial uses permitted by copyright law.

Printed in the United States of America Copyright 2024© Koso Brown

Contents

Introduction 1

Chapter 1 3

So, What Exactly Is Lean and Lean Marketing? 3

Chapter 2 8

What Distinguishes Traditional Marketing from the Lean Marketing Framework? 8

Chapter 3 13

Lean marketing strategy 13

Chapter 4 24

What benefits does lean marketing offer? 24

Chapter 5 31

How to build a Lean Sales funnel from Scratch 31

Chapter 6 37

Why 1-1-1 Product Launching Is Effective 37

Conclusion 39

Introduction

The marketing landscape is changing. It's growing in significance, becoming more tech-focused, expanding into new disciplines, and integrating with other departments more than before.

Most teams find it very impossible to plan activities and campaigns within realistic and predictable periods because the day-to-day work in marketing is so varied and dynamic, which is pretty much why we love it. Instead, most teams rely on agencies, partners, and consultants from outside sources. We are aware that marketing needs a fresh look to complement its strong personality to boost productivity and turn complicated assignments into manageable chores.

Although "lean marketing" is more frequently associated with startups, all marketing campaigns have a budget, regardless of whether you're marketing for a massive corporation like Google or a neighborhood pizzeria.

Lean marketing is more than simply an attention-grabbing way of saying low-cost, accessible, within budget, doable, and feasible.

We will get into the definitions of lean and lean marketing in this reading.

Continuous improvement, consumer input (often in smaller batches), and flexible marketing staff are all essential components of lean marketing.

When you work for a small business, determining what is financially feasible will heavily influence your marketing techniques.

Small business owners rely on a lean marketing approach to maximize their marketing budget and increase their marketing efforts. They put marketing concepts and workflows into practice to provide better outcomes more quickly.

Can a lean strategy be used while still implementing your marketing ideas? Of course! Creating ideas that have an effect doesn't require a large expense. You need a method that you have tried and proven to be effective.

Chapter 1

So, What Exactly Is Lean and Lean Marketing?

The Toyota Way, commonly referred to as the Manufacturing System (TMS), is the source of lean management philosophy. As a result of its great success, American automakers eventually adopted the idea. It was only available to businesses engaged in the production of goods and products for a long time before Eric Ries started conducting tests based on the lean philosophy approximately ten years ago.

In his book "The Lean Startup," Eric provides a more thorough breakdown of how these ideas assisted him in creating the virtual avatar platform IMVU. Lean methodology's basic tenets are to act more quickly, iterate more often, and provide value without wasting time or resources, according to various Lean resources. Although the software development and manufacturing sectors are currently where lean is most commonly applied, I'm sure that marketing may also benefit from it.

Lean Marketing

There's a good reason why lean marketing has started to gain popularity recently! Because of the nature of their work, most marketers must continually shift their goals and areas of concentration; the dynamic nature of our industry doesn't make it any easier. Without a doubt, we need a framework to increase productivity without interfering with our creative process.

It is partially accurate to assume that the Lean marketing framework is the well-known model of Acquisition, Activation, Retention, Referral, and Revenue. The manner a marketing team operates and measures is what distinguishes a lean team.

Lean marketing strategy is the key to achieving incalculable outcomes. We all understand that you can't improve anything if you can't measure it. However, thanks to empirical data and scientific analysis, we now have the chance to turn our process into a tool that lets us affect outcomes. Measurable results and data-driven analysis take the role of guesswork and estimation.

Any lean marketing framework's guiding principles

Using Lean Thinking

The marketing team as a whole is affected by this, beginning with the team lead. You aim to inculcate fundamental ideas like effect over everything, 80/20, and a lean mindset. One cannot enhance something if it is not measurable. Data are vital to lean firms.

Most marketers have a few tricks up their sleeve; they are adept at doing a lot with little, which is a useful ability in a startup that is being funded entirely by bootstrapping. Lean creation processes should be the foundation of the process: figure it out. Use your imagination. Make use of what you have. Bring it about. Don't go over budget.

Innovative marketing campaigns

A lean organization is aware of how important it is to maintain flexibility. A key distinction between a lean approach and traditional marketing is that the latter begins with an idea, proceeds through a protracted process, and evaluates its performance at the conclusion.

The lean startup model places a greater emphasis on campaign insights, offering the opportunity to make adjustments mid-campaign if doing so will ultimately improve the campaign's success. Perfect concepts are not necessary for the lean startup movement; instead, it require lean marketers who can make swift adjustments based on consumer findings.

Process effectiveness

Agile marketing enables plan revisions with the use of measurement instruments to find the best course of action. An efficient process releases the product as quickly as possible to gather feedback, cut down on waste, and, if required, make any necessary direction changes. Small firms are unable to finance expensive, ineffective marketing initiatives. Perhaps more regular status meetings will be necessary as a result, but if it increases ROI, isn't that worth it?

What advantages does a lean marketing approach offer?

Optimal results for your lean startup

You can have a preferred marketing channel based on your industry or niche. Lean small business owners encourage their marketing managers to test concepts in small batches to determine which would produce the best outcomes.

Rather than allocating your budget to a single marketing channel, you experiment on multiple platforms, determine which one works best, and then focus your team's efforts and resources on value-adding initiatives.

Customized marketing communications

The marketing messages are customized to the demands of the customer, reader, or target audience because lean marketing mainly depends on customer insights not just at the start or finish of the campaign, but also throughout.

Lean startups do more measuring and less guesswork

Measuring data is a crucial component of this whole idea. Utilize app analytics to track user behavior and get continuous learning. Going skinny does not mean going blind. Data is used by marketing teams who adopt a lean methodology to make decisions.

Chapter 2

What Distinguishes Traditional Marketing from the Lean Marketing Framework?

In traditional marketing, teams are unable to modify and adapt during the development process because the end product is predetermined in the marketing strategy or plan. Marketing experts occasionally begin to repeat specific actions indefinitely without consistently gauging their success. Consumer attention fluctuates, and they frequently lose interest when they receive communications that are not perfectly tailored to them or that lack originality.

This is where the most important Lean tenets can be found: constant testing and learning, never taking a positive trend for granted, and a constant pursuit of excellence.

Lean marketing depends on the following essential elements to be implemented:

Fulfill more quickly.

Large, long-term deliverables should be broken down into smaller jobs. Deliver the smaller components every few weeks and iterate until the best solution is found. I always prefer fast over sluggish. You start working on smaller batches when you limit the amount of work you're working on, and as a result, you can see the results of your labor sooner. If we apply that to a marketing campaign, then you will be able to test and launch them more quickly. Fast iterations are the other facet of speed. The Build>>Measure>>Learn loop is one of Eric Ries's fundamental ideas. Iterating several times allows you to significantly enhance each cycle relative to the last.

Regular status meetings
to talk about what's done, what's working, and what's preventing your team from accomplishing more (feedback loops). Start by holding daily stand-up meetings. These are quick team get-togethers, lasting no more than 15 minutes, whose purpose is to keep everyone in the team informed of each other's activities. Each participant is required to give the following information: what they did the day before, what they want to do today, and any obstacles they have encountered or anticipate. Having regular stand-ups is crucial to transforming your marketing team into a lean operation.

In addition to keeping your team together at all times, they assist you in identifying and resolving member difficulties before they become issues. Encouraging peer-to-peer learning is one of the most beneficial aspects of daily stand-ups, as it is essential to the success of any organization.

Remain concentrated

People are encouraged to concentrate and work on single tasks by the Lean marketing strategy. Here, multitasking is frowned upon since it merely deters from being productive. One of the main components of Lean is focus, which you may further improve with Kanban. When working on two activities at once, you will complete them much more quickly than if you work on them concurrently.

That's the reason multitasking is ineffective! However, the reality is somewhat different, particularly when interacting with individuals. You eventually have to switch between several activities because there is always something more important to perform, but this doesn't imply you can't optimize the process. ongoing development. Recall? Limiting the amount of work in progress will help you finish tasks more quickly by reducing the need to transfer between contexts.

Avoid making your strategy absolute.

This situation exemplifies Eisenhower's adage, "Plans are nothing; planning is everything." Plans are useful because they provide direction for the team, but being Lean means being adaptable, so you need to strike the correct balance between carrying out the plan to the letter and mindlessly adhering to it. Within Eric Ries's technique, this is referred to as "pivoting." Data must support your decision to change course or stay in your existing position; it cannot be made on the spur of the moment.

Components of a Lean Marketing Strategy

Alright. We refer to it as a strategy because implementing a lean marketing process is a calculated decision that will fundamentally alter the way your team operates. A few components are common to lean marketing. Being aware of them from the start will make it easier for you to incorporate them into the way your process is currently operating. Lean suggests that you start with what you do now, without making any annoying modifications. Utilize what you already have and add to it little by little.

- ❖ **Personas.** Decide who you want to interact with. This removes the possibility of taking part in pointless, untargeted communications.

- ❖ **A marketing procedure** that supports iteration and analytics.

- ❖ **Measurement.** Analytics for websites or applications that track user interactions and activity.

- ❖ **Instruments for measuring and testing.** To test and validate messages, designs, and concepts, marketing process automation, A/B testing, and lifecycle tracking are used.

- ❖ **An improved launch and publication approval procedure.** Iteration is a constant in lean marketing. Create modest concepts, launch them into the market, assess the response, gain knowledge, and then iterate with the insights gained.

Chapter 3

Lean marketing strategy

Set goals

Without objectives, launching a marketing campaign is like sprinting in the dark. You will inevitably trip and fall.

Clearly define the objectives you hope to accomplish with the campaign. S.M.A.R.T. goals are one of the most well-known frameworks to assist you with it.

S: Be specific. Don't, for example, state that your goal is to generate 10 new leads every month. Instead, let them know that you're looking for ten leads from B2B SaaS providers. Isn't that incredibly clear and specific?

M: Your goals should be measurable. How will you assess your outcomes if you are unable to measure them?

A: Make sure you can achieve your goals with the given resources. Avoid going beyond your limits.

R: Don't set out-of-the-world goals. Establish realistic goals to avoid disappointment on the road.

T: Define a deadline to reach each goal. That will encourage you to continue working toward your goal. Avoid going beyond your limits.

R: Avoid having impossible aims. Establish realistic goals to avoid disappointment on the road.

T: Establish a deadline for completing each task. That will encourage you to continue working toward your goal.

Brainstorm

Optimization of the campaign for your customers is the goal of lean marketing. It makes an effort to reduce superfluous stuff. Hence, brainstorming with your groups would assist you in producing creative concepts that could appeal to your intended market. You can evaluate your consumer insights and modify your campaign by using brainstorming techniques.

Clarify ideas

Your marketing ideas ought to be very apparent. That will guarantee your campaign's success.

You won't be able to generate original campaign ideas until you have a firm grasp of all the theoretical notions.

Publicize and gather information
Go ahead and launch your campaign after spending those many hours coming up with ideas. Ensure that you keep an eye on the feedback and outcomes. You must gather all of your performance data since doing so will enable you to determine whether the campaign is effective. To obtain precise data, a variety of analytics techniques are available.

Determine the insights from business intelligence analysis.
Your past and current data are examined by business intelligence insights to provide you with useful information. You learn about current events as well as how things have operated in the past. As a result, you can determine what needs to be altered for better performance. By examining business intelligence information, you can gain insight into customer behavior. As a result, you will be able to tailor your marketing initiatives to the interests and problems of your target audience

Here are some pointers for mastering lean marketing strategies with business intelligence insights:

- ❖ Employ analytics programs

- ❖ Based on the analytics, make business judgments.

- ❖ Utilizing dashboards and visualizations, interpreting data

Fine-tune and repeat

Repetition and learning are the cornerstones of lean marketing. It's time to make adjustments and run your campaign again after you have thoroughly examined all of the data and analytics. Your campaign will perform far better now that you have gained insight from your errors. Additionally, it will be customized to your client's requirements and preferences.

What are the principles of lean marketing?

Lean marketing works on the following principles:

Quick delivery is the top priority.

The secret is to provide value to the customer as quickly as feasible. The main long-term deliverables are divided into smaller ones by lean marketers. Delivery times are accelerated as a result.

The idea is to fail quickly so that you may use the lessons you learn to improve your campaigns. It takes little time to gather input and make the required adjustments because the deliverables are brief. Use an hour's tracker to see how long your jobs are taking so you can deliver them more quickly. That will assist you in making better plans for increased productivity.

Regular feedback sessions are essential.
Every lean marketing strategy must include regular feedback sessions. They support teams in examining what is and is not effective. As a result, you learn what adjustments are necessary to make your campaign better. Every step of the marketing process is continuously scrutinized. Errors are therefore difficult to conceal. For example, you must continuously assess the performance of your social media postings and blogs if you use content marketing. Gatherings facilitate that.

Marketers need to focus on one thing at a time.
Lean marketing allows you to concentrate on a single objective rather than multitasking because it demands smaller deliverables. That will increase the output of your team.

When multiple jobs are completed at once, the quality of the finished product suffers. However, you receive great quality and expedite the completion of your work when you narrow down your emphasis.

Assume you are working on two projects at once. If you take each one by itself, you'll finish them more quickly.

Every plan is adjustable.
Avoid establishing firm plans. Who knows what the circumstances will hold? Rather, keep your plans flexible to allow for any necessary modifications. Let's take an example where you planned a large-scale marketing campaign and spent a significant chunk of money on it. But what happens if the strategy is being implemented

and the market conditions change? It is therefore always preferable to have flexible strategies. In this manner, if your strategy fails, you won't get into any difficulties.

Every component needs to be kept on hand at all times. It is obvious how to use this approach. If you don't have everything ready, you can't move quickly. These are a few of those "things" to think about:

A. Multiple buyer personas

Who are the perfect clients for you? You may have a variety of clientele. Therefore, creating many buyer personas is preferable. You may then use that to make your campaigns more unique.
Creating buyer personas requires an understanding of your target audience. Don't, however, restrict your understanding to their geography, gender, or age. Go far further to learn about their most private goals and struggles.

Your marketing strategy will be more successful the more you comprehend the psychology of your target audience.

So, how are your buyer personas created?

Step 1: Gather as much data as you can on your customer base. This ought to cover their objectives, problems, and difficulties. Learn about their daily routines and financial situation as well.

Step 2: Divide up your customer base based on their area, interests, gender, age, and location. Not every client will fall into the same category.

Step 3: Name your buyer personas and include a photo in each one. You can then add even more personalization to it.

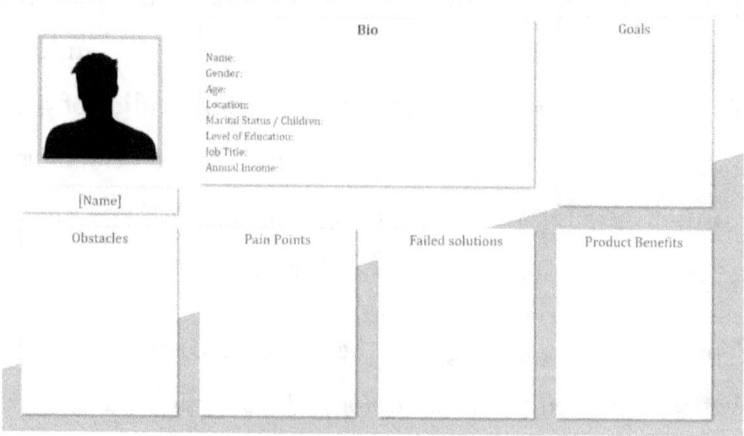

B. A well-defined procedure for marketing development

A well-defined and unambiguous marketing approach is important to ensure the triumph of your campaign. Ensure that your approach allows for iteration and analytics. Analytics can provide you with in-depth knowledge about the preferences of your clients. Also, you will comprehend the effectiveness of your advertising. You can therefore repeat the procedure after making the required adjustment Replicability should be a part of your marketing development process. To ensure that your campaign is customized to your client's preferences, you may need to repeat it with a few minor adjustments.

C. Tools for conversion and analytics

You can track customer activity with the use of analytics and conversion tools. Take the way your clients are interacting with your campaigns, for example. To what extent are they clicking on your posts? What is the ratio of conversion? You may use all of this information to gauge how well your lean marketing plan is working. Most social media platforms come with analytics features by default. Conversion tools are another useful tool for understanding consumer behavior.

D. A cohesive team

Without a cohesive team, plans, procedures, and equipment are useless. Your marketing staff will carry out the tactical execution of your campaigns.

Ensure that the members are properly coordinating with one another. The secret to mastering a lean marketing strategy is effective communication.

Keep in mind that there will be a lot of little deliverables. Moreover, the process will involve ongoing assessment and modification. As a result, your marketing team should have a great working connection with other professionals and have access to online resources to help them improve.

Your team members' ability to communicate clearly and have a growth mindset will determine the success of your lean strategy.

E. A procedure involving multiple people for approval

The process of lean marketing is iterative. You pitch your ideas to the market, get feedback, apply what you've learned, and then start the cycle again. Therefore, more than one person should be able to approve your proposals. Adhere to a multidisciplinary approval process. This will assist you in verifying if your campaign is appropriate for your intended audience. It will also assist you in navigating the various adjustments that you must make.

Chapter 4

What benefits does lean marketing offer?

Let's examine a few of the advantages of lean marketing.

- ❖ **Fast delivery.** Larger tasks are divided into manageable chunks by lean marketers. You receive the finished product faster as a result of the improved turnaround time.
- ❖ **Improves setting priorities.** The goal of lean marketing is to cut waste. As a result, you tend to overlook the little things and concentrate on what matters.

  Knowing your priorities will also make your marketing campaigns more memorable. Additionally, data and input are the foundations of your decisions. You therefore know exactly what your plan has to contain.
- ❖ **Increases output.** Using a lean approach keeps your staff engaged. You cannot afford to overlook any small aspect of your campaigns' performance. All team members must thus maintain constant alertness.

  Collaborative planning (such as using the Kanban

method) and clear communication among team members are also essential components of lean marketing. Every team member must be knowledgeable about how the campaigns are performing.

Your team becomes extremely productive through continuous learning, application of knowledge, and iteration.

❖ **Keep your company's customers in mind.** According to lean marketing, you must continuously modify your tactics to suit the needs of your target audience. As a result, you attract more clients and your company gains credibility. You continuously adjust your campaigns in response to consumer input. This implies that every one of your marketing messages will be extremely tailored. After all, if you don't target the correct customers, no marketing approach will be successful.

How Can Lean Marketing Be Initiated?

Adopting Lean requires a group effort to pursue small, gradual improvements. The best outcomes can only be achieved via mutual discussion and agreement. Establishing frequent feedback loops, such as a daily stand-up meeting, weekly KPI meetings, and monthly strategy meetings, is the next stage. They must be brief, have a clear agenda, and be followed by specified takeaways. Lean mostly involves a shift in people's perspectives.

The Kanban approach is the simplest way to incorporate Lean ideas into your business. Kanban is simple to use and strives for tiny, gradual improvements. It includes useful instructions and equipment to utilize. When you visualize all of your work on a Kanban board, you can track each task's progress from Requested to Done and identify any bottlenecks in your workflow. The traditional physical whiteboard with cards is still in use, but these days you can also start kanbanizing your workflow relatively easily with online boards.

One of the greatest Lean/Agile PPM platforms Kanban software packages that fully integrates Kanban into your marketing endeavors is Kanbanizing by Business Map. To maximize its application in terms of visualization, work-in-progress restrictions, role distribution, task prioritizing, and flow analysis, it extends every Kanban principle. You can simply monitor the progress of each assignment and keep track of major campaigns with ease using the Portfolio lane.

For management that isn't often active in a given project regularly, this may save a ton of time.

The majority of the information shared by marketing teams with other departments and outside parties, including partners, agencies, etc., is sent by email. Marketing teams are always in communication and coordination with these groups. You can import and track all of your chores at once with online Kanban boards by integrating them with other systems and your emails. Adding deadlines to cards and using the Business rules engine to set reminders is a smart way to make sure nothing gets behind schedule.

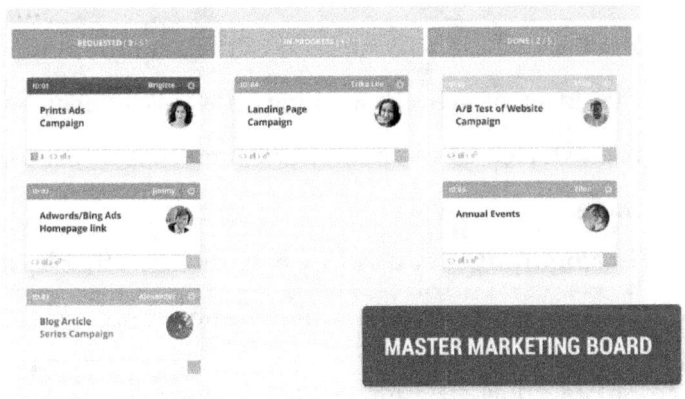

A lean marketing board example

Metrics for Tracking Lean Marketing Success

To ensure success, if you are unsure about which indicators to monitor, here are the top four lean metrics you should measure:

- ❖ **WIP:** the total number of work items that are deemed to be in progress at any given time or within a specific time.
- ❖ **Cycle Time:** the amount of time it takes for your chores to be completed.
- ❖ **Process efficiency**: the ratio of the amount of time that is spent actively working on a task after it has been started to the amount of time that it just sits there.
- ❖ **Throughput:** the quantity of work items that leave your system in a predetermined amount of time.

The cumulative flow diagram, or CFD for short, is a favorite tool of many Lean practitioners and one of the tools you may use to keep an eye on them. It provides a succinct visual representation of the cycle duration, throughput, and work-in-progress characteristics of flow. Large volumes of information can be synthesized and presented understandably with only a glance at the cumulative flow diagram.

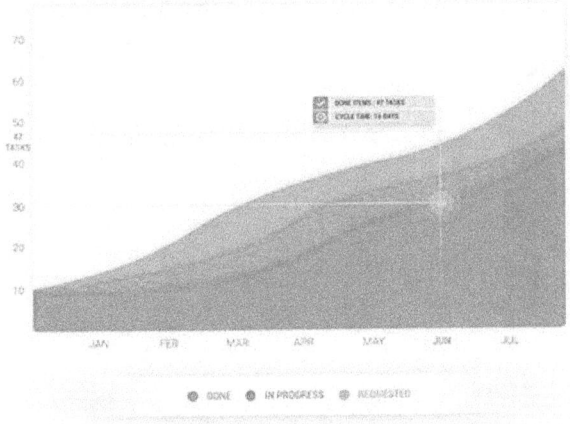

Cumulative flow diagram example

Predictive Monte Carlo simulations are another very helpful tool to add to your analytics toolbox. They can predict how many work items you could complete in a certain amount of time or when several jobs will be completed. A practical and statistically sound method of characterizing uncertainty in the variables of a risk analysis is using probability distributions. They give you and your team and stakeholders the ability to make data-driven decisions. This makes it possible for marketing teams to set deadlines based on likelihood rather than wishful thinking.

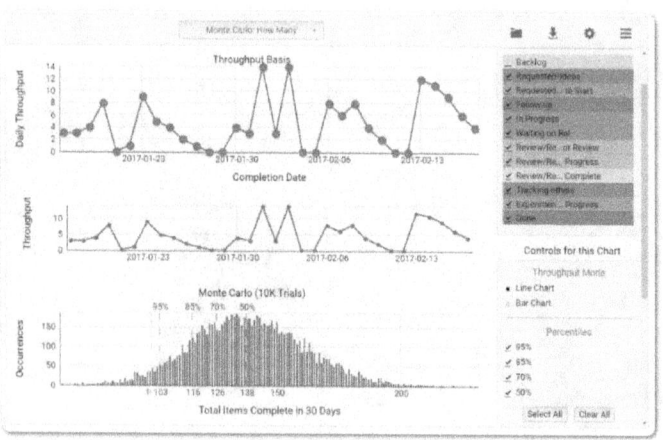

What's to Come in the First Three Months?

- ❖ Significant improvement in efficiency.
- ❖ Members of remote teams participate more actively in the work process and assume greater accountability and initiative.
- ❖ Better dialogue and a reduction in "he said, she said" as all the information is displayed on the board.
- ❖ No more data loss.

❖ Promoted knowledge exchange to achieve ongoing improvement.

Chapter 5

How to build a Lean sales funnel from scratch

Let's define the lean marketing funnel's five steps as follows:

Revenue, Acquisition, Activation, Retention, and Referral.

Acquisition: attract visitors to your site

Activation: get this person to take action (free trial, newsletter subscription, etc.)

Retention: entice this visitor to return to your website several times (for example, by sending them a newsletter or by having them use their free trial).

Referral: Persuade this person to tell others about it, directly or indirectly. Examples include word-of-mouth marketing, which is done directly, and software branding, which increases the likelihood that people will click on your logo when they see it.

Revenues: persuade the user to purchase something (your book, an upgraded version of your software, a premium course or training program, etc.).

These same elements that are utilized to design lean sales funnels are also used to build lean marketing funnels for our newest product, which I'll tell you about below.

Steer Clear of Complexity in Your Sales Funnel

There are countless methods to overdo the online sales process; you can accentuate your product or service, add bells and whistles to your advertising, and add features to your sales page. You may invest weeks developing the greatest survey lead magnet ever (been there, done that), days crafting the greatest graphics, or months developing "virality" into your product.

Ultimately, all of this merely serves to overcomplicate everything.

The ease of handling the entire procedure is just as important to the launch's success as the caliber of the good or service and the efficiency of the sales funnel. "User error" is the main cause of product launch failures.

Put simply, the system gets more complex the more components or layers we add to the funnel. The consequences of complexity
In the best scenario, you created a Rube Goldberg machine. The worst case—which occurs more frequently—is that it fails.

What then is the substitute?
a straightforward sales funnel that converts visitors into devoted clients.
Here it is the 1-1-1 Product Launch Process.

The 1-1-1 Product Launch Method: How to Simplify and Optimize Your Sales Funnel

A straightforward method for implementing the previously described lean marketing funnel to launch a single good or service is the 1-1-1 Product Launch Method.

By concentrating solely on the fundamentals and eliminating waste, the 1-1-1 Product Launch Method eliminates the need for an unduly complicated funnel.

There are three (surprise!) essential components that make

up the 1-1-1 Product Launch Method:

- ❖ Just one lead generator (the thing that drives traffic to your site)
- ❖ One splash page, or the page you direct potential clients to
- ❖ A single conversion process that converts website visitors into devoted patrons

One Lead Generator

Finding a single strategy to generate leads for your product or service is the ideal approach if you're seeking to build an efficient sales funnel. Although there are several methods to attract clients, you'll need to focus and narrow your efforts unless you work for a big firm or have a lot of extra cash. This is especially true if you're just starting.

It is much better to concentrate on just ONE lead generation source so you can become extremely skilled at it, rather than spreading yourself too thin and producing a lot of things that don't work. It makes no sense to try to drive traffic from a podcast, Facebook ads, outbound marketing, and affiliates right at the beginning.

One Splash Page

All of your efforts ought to direct readers to a single page. Just one page.

Just one (and there's no need to even split test this); not two, not five, not ten.

This page should make sense both in terms of the message that first drew users to it and in terms of the conversion the procedure you plan to employ. Thus, the one splash page should be a webinar option page if your goal is to convert visitors through a sales webinar, for instance. Additionally, visitors to your website from your lead generator have to be aware that they are going to a page where they may sign up for a webinar.

It's important to remain constant throughout.

One Conversion Procedure

Avoid attempting to market a product in a dozen ways. Just concentrate on converting site visitors into devoted clients. The conversion process in the webinar scenario would be a sales webinar—not a free e-course, not directing them to a static sales page, but making a sale to them during the webinar.

Conversion process examples include:

- ❖ Unchanging sales page

- ❖ Automated reply with upsells
- ❖ In-person gathering or occasion
- ❖ A live webinar concluding with a sales pitch
- ❖ Skype call or phone call

The least successful sales page is most likely one that is static. Numerous business owners with audiences of over 10,000 have told me about their product or service launches. They had hoped that a straightforward sales page would increase sales, but instead, the conversion rate was less than 1% (i.e., less than 1% of 10,000 visitors = 100 sales, which is not very much for a list that size). Conversion then surged when they added a live webcast, phone calls, and other more active conversion methods to the mix.

Chapter 6

Why 1-1-1 Product Launching Is Effective

First of all, it prioritizes learning and progress. How do you tell what is effective and ineffective when you are experimenting with a dozen various strategies to market your good or service? However, if you concentrate on a single thing, you can measure it accurately and conclude it.

And success is inexorably linked to learning. Secondly, it's doable.

As I previously stated, user error accounts for the majority of launch failures. Frequently as a result of an overly intricate launch procedure.

Simplicity is the cornerstone of the 1-1-1 Product Launch Method. This strategy is feasible for a single person working part-time.

What Happens If There Is No Audience?

Now, the premise behind this strategy is that you are speaking to an audience.

However, what if you don't?

You construct one, then.

Before we had our first sales webinar, we had to spend some money on targeted Facebook advertisements to compile a list of more than 200 people.

For you, that can mean using a tool like Untorch.com to disseminate your message virally (is that even a word?), sharing your work with interested Facebook groups, or sharing it with family and friends. it is now).

In the end, you require a viewership.

The good news is that building one doesn't require much.

Conclusion

Using lean marketing strategies saves your business time. Its main tenets include adaptability, data tracking, and failing quickly to guarantee a marketing plan's success. Lessons acquired via a traditional marketing campaign are still obtained, but they are learned more quickly and provide you more time to adjust the course if needed. Ship more quickly. Having tested your tiny concepts in the relevant market, you should have a clear agenda early in the campaign.

Your company grows because of your customers. If your marketing campaigns aren't adapted to the interests and problems of your target audience, what good are they? By delivering tailored campaigns, going lean improves your chances of success.

So, prepare for a higher return on investment from your marketing budget by becoming lean now.

www.ingramcontent.com/pod-product-compliance
Lightning Source LLC
Chambersburg PA
CBHW070951220526
45471CB00007B/2990